Phonics

This workbook belongs to

Use pencils, crayons, and stickers to complete the activities in this book. When there is a sticker missing, you will see this pattern:

The wh sound

Say the words. Circle **wh** in each word.

wheel

whistle

whale

wheat

Read the question words aloud.
Circle the one that doesn't start with **wh**.

when why

what

how which

The wr sound

Say the words. Circle **wr** in each word.

wrench

wrap

write

wrong

Say each word and write **wr**.

wrist

wring

wreck

wren

ph and gh

Say the words. Circle **ph** in **pink** and **gh** in **blue**.

phone

rough

photo

tough

Say each word and trace **ph** or **gh**.

laugh

dolphin

trophy

cough

gn and kn

Say the words. Circle **gn** in **red** and **kn** in **purple**.

gnome

knight

sign

knife

Say each word and trace **gn** or **kn**.

gnaw

knit

knob

gnu

ch and tch

Say the words. Circle **ch** in **blue** and **tch** in **red**.

catch

march

peach

watch

Say each word and trace **ch** or **tch**.

hatch

lunch

bench

match

ng and nk

Say the words. Circle **ng** in **orange** and **nk** in **pink**.

king

pink

drink

gong

Say each word and trace **ng** or **nk**.

wing

wink

hang

bunk

sh and th

Say the words. Circle **sh** in **blue** and **th** in **red**.

thumb

ship

fish

teeth

 Say each word and trace **sh** or **th**.

brush

three 3

moth

sheep

br and bl

Say the words. Circle br in orange and bl in green.

bread

blocks

blanket

branch

Say each word and trace **br** or **bl**.

blink

bridge

blue

broom

Silent e

A **silent e** makes the other vowel say its name.
The other vowel goes from **short** to **long**.
Say the words and trace the vowels.

 man | mane

 pet | Pete

pin | pine

hop | hope

 cub | cube

Silent e practice

Circle the correct word.

tap
(tape)

rat
rate

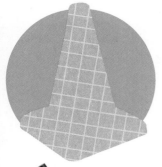
hat
hate

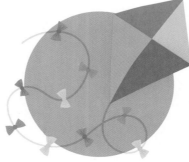
kit
kite

con
cone

rid
ride

glob
globe

hug
huge

cut
cute

tub
tube

Bossy r words

When **r** comes after a vowel, the vowel sound changes.
Circle the words with **ar** in them in **blue**.
Circle the words with **or** in them in **red**.
Then draw lines to match each word to its picture.

car
fork
barn
horn
harp
corn
shark
horse
star
storm

More bossy r words

Say the words. Trace the **er** sound in each word.
It is spelled three ways here.

 surf

girl

 fern

turkey

 water

bird

 nurse

baker

Write two other ways **er** is spelled here.

er

The oy sound

Say the words. Trace the **oy** sound in each word.
It is spelled two ways here.

coin

boy

joy

noisy

Circle the letters that make the **oy** sound.

point

annoy

toy

toilet

The long a sound

Say the words. Trace the **long a** sound in each word.
It is spelled three ways here.

  cake sail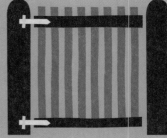

 hay mail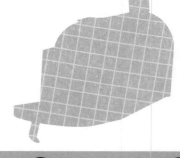

 train gate

 wave tray

Write two other ways **long a** is spelled here.

 a-e

The long e sound

Say the words. Trace the **long e** sound in each word.
It is spelled four ways here.

bee

thief

puppy

peas

Circle the letters that make the **long e** sound.

cheese

shield

twenty 20

seal

The long i sound

Say the words. Trace the **long i** sound in each word.
It is spelled four ways here.

pie

fly

cry

tie

bike

spy

tights

knight

Write three other ways **long i** is spelled here.

i-e

The long o sound

Say the words. Trace the **long o** sound in each word.
It is spelled two ways here.

boat

row

yellow

soap

Circle the letters that make the **long o** sound.

coat

bow

mow

toast

The ow sound

Say the words. Trace the **ow** sound in each word.
It is spelled two ways here.

house   cow

howl   mouse

crown   cloud

owl   shout

Write two ways the **ow** sound is spelled here.

The long oo sound

Say the words. Trace the **long oo** sound in each word.
It is spelled four ways here.

moose

blue

tube

chew

 Circle the letters that make the **long oo** sound.

goose

glue

rude

stew

Long oo and short oo

Say **zoo**. Circle the words with this **long oo** sound in **purple**.
Say **book**. Circle the words with this **short oo** sound in green.
Then draw lines to match each word to its picture.

Woof!

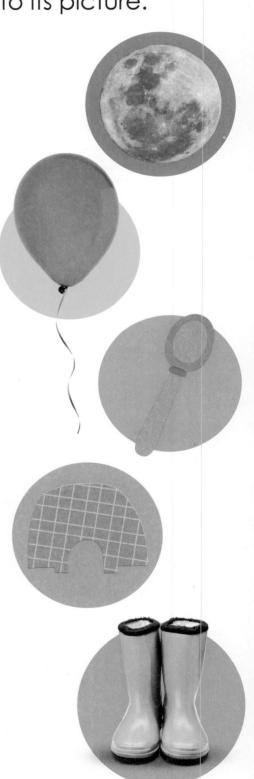

woof

moon

wood

igloo

cookie

boots

foot

spoon

hook

balloon

The aw sound

Say the words. Trace the **aw** sound in each word.
It is spelled four ways here.

fork

door

yawn

ball

Circle the letters that make the **aw** sound.

horse

poor

paw

walk

The air sound

Say the words. Trace the **air** sound in each word.
It is spelled three ways here.

pair

hare

bear

square

 Circle the letters that make the **air** sound.

chair

share

pear

tear

Congratulations!

GOOD WORK AWARD!

Name: ....

has successfully completed the

Kindergarten
Phonics Workbook.

Date: ....

Search this page for the stickers you need.

Pages **2–3**

Pages **4–5**

Pages **6–7**

Pages **8–9**

Pages **10–11**

Pages **12–13**

Pages **14–15**

Pages **16–17**

Pages **18–19**

Pages **20–21**

Pages **22–23**

Certificate stickers